Roy went to the fun park.
He went with Grandad.

Roy was hungry.
Grandad was hungry too.

They had a hot dog.

They went on the cable car.

'What a ride!' said Grandad.

They went on the water splash.

'Oh no!' said Roy.

They had an ice-cream.

They had a drink.

They went on the rockets.

‘Oh help!’ said Grandad.

They had some chips.

Roy wanted some popcorn.

They went on the space boat.

'Oh help!' said Roy.
'What a ride!' said Grandad.

Roy had a lollipop.

Grandad had some candy floss.

They went on the corkscrew.

Grandad was frightened.
Roy was frightened too.

‘Oh no!’ said Grandad.
‘Oh help!’ said Roy.

They got out.

Roy felt sick.

Grandad felt sick too.